The Book of
LIES

The Book of
LIES

MARY KANE

First published in Great Britain in 2001 by
Michael O'Mara Books Limited
9 Lion Yard
Tremadoc Road
London SW4 7NQ

Copyright © Michael O'Mara Books Ltd 2001

A CIP catalogue record for this book is available from the British Library

ISBN 1-85479-185-0

1 3 5 7 9 10 8 6 4 2

Designed and typeset by Design 23

Printed and bound in Great Britain by Cox and Wyman, Reading, Berks.

CONTENTS

Once upon
there was

a time, great liar

Headline *The Times*, 20th July 2001
On the 'rollercoaster' life of
Lord Archer of Weston-super-Mare

The First Lie?

'I do not know; am I my brother's keeper?'

Cain – to God, denying any knowledge of the
whereabouts of his brother, Abel, after killing him.

(Genesis 4:9)

KANE AND ABEL

keeping it in the family

'LIE FATHER... LIE SON'

'He bragged that his dad had been a colonel in the Somerset Light Infantry and had been awarded the Distinguished Conduct Medal for gallantry. When the claim was exposed as bogus, Archer was forced to resign from the society for holders of the DCM and their offspring.'

Headline and extract from the *Sun*, 20th July 2001, on Lord Archer

Ten lies between brothers

1 I just want one little bite
2 That scary sound is not coming from next door
3 Dad won't mind
4 Who do you think they'll believe?
5 I won't let anything happen to you
6 I've done it millions of times, I swear it
7 I'll be right behind you
8 You're not really my brother
9 Mum and Dad love me more than you
10 I'll do it for the next week, if you just do it today

...his c.v. b

Sandhurst,

California.

all just fa

asted of

Oxford and

but it was

asy

Headline in the *Mirror* 20th July 2001
on Lord Archer of Weston-super-Mare

Ten lies parents tell their children

1   We won't be angry, just tell us the truth
2   We love all our children the same
3   This hurts us more than it hurts you
4   Of course we trust you
5   In the future you'll thank us for this
6   You can always tell us the truth
7   It'll happen, you just have to wait
8   It's not a question of money
9   Your brother/sister never behaved like this
10 Just close your eyes; you don't have to go to sleep

Almost 90 years before Lord Archer faced an Old Bailey jury, William Archer, his father, appeared in the same court, in October 1914. He was accused of fraud, obtaining money by false pretences and unlawfully getting credit. The case was adjourned for four weeks and he was bailed. He skipped the country and fled to America where he pretended to be raising money for a charity to buy artificial limbs for French soldiers. In 1917, he was jailed for three years. He got probation and fled to Canada, where he was soon in trouble again for tricking a widow out of her war bonds. A sentence of three year's hard labour was commuted to deportation.

James Arch

a liar by city

branded
watchdog

Ten more lies parents tell their children

1   It's not what you look like that matters; it's who you are on the inside
2   I'm not going to lose my temper
3   Your rabbit has gone to rabbit heaven
4   No one will be looking at you
5   I'm sure there will be lots of other children there
6   I found it when I was tidying your room
7   It isn't a matter of win or lose; it's how you play the game
8   You'll grow into it (or out of it)
9   Of course I'm listening
10 When you're older

'James Archer, the son of disgraced Lord Archer of Weston-super-Mare was branded a liar by City regulators. Archer, 27, received an indefinite ban from working in the City and was ordered to pay costs of £50,000 for a blatant attempt to manipulate the Swedish Stock Exchange. The ban came just a week after his father was sentenced to four years in jail for perjury and attempting to pervert the course of justice. The charges levelled against James come from his days as one of the 'Flaming Ferraris', a notorious group of City traders named after the strong cocktail they used to drink on Friday nights.'

Evening Standard, 27th July 2001

' "George," said his father, "Do you know who killed this beautiful little cherry tree yonder in the garden?"
"I can't tell a lie, Pa; you know I can't tell a lie. I did cut it with my hatchet." '

In 1806 biographer Mason Weems fabricated this most famous of all lies and presented it in his biography of President George Washington. This was in fact only one of countless false anecdotes, which he used to pad his poorly researched life of the President

Education,
Education,
Education.

'Lord Archer's father, William Archer, 'laced his lies [in US during the First World War] with bogus tales of his schooldays at Eton and medical studies at Oxford University.'

FIRST AMONG EQUALS

birds of a feather?

'I was not lying. I said things that later on seemed to be untrue.'

Former US President Richard Nixon, 1978, some four years after the Watergate scandal forced his resignation

'When he won a seat on the Greater London Council in 1967, he claimed to be the youngest ever GLC councillor, but he was two years older than Anthony Bradbury, elected at the same time. He tried it again in 1969, when he was elected MP for Louth at 29. Archer described himself as "the youngest member of the House of Commons", overlooking the fact that Bernadette Devlin was 22 at the time.'

The *Mirror*, 20th July 2001,
on Lord Archer of Weston-super-Mare

'No one in the White House Staff, no one in this administration, presently employed, was involved in this very bizarre incident.'

1972: US President Richard Nixon, lying to the American public at the outset of the Watergate scandal

'[In 1967]...Archer, displaying his flair for
creativity, helped his fellow Tory
Councillors to fill in their expense claim
forms for a 10 per cent commission. Even
this relatively innocent practice was
swathed in lies.'

Andrew Pierce *The Times*, 20th July 2001

'He threatened legal action when this accusation appeared in Michael Crick's biography,
Stranger Than Fiction.
'However Crick found 24 former councillors who recalled Archer doing this, and six who confirmed he did it for them.'

Daily Mail, 20th July 2001

'Approximately 80 per cent of air pollution stems from hydrocarbons released by vegetation, so let's not go overboard in setting and enforcing tough emission standards from manmade sources.'

Former US President Ronald Reagan: In 1981, President Reagan, anxious to appease his many campaign contributors in the motor industry, claimed that trees caused more air pollution than motor cars

'On September 8th 1986, a man entered the Albion Hotel in Victoria with prostitute Monica Coughlan. The driver of a parked blue Mercedes car, Aziz Kartha, believed he recognized the man as Jeffrey Archer and contacted the *News of the World.* On October 26th 1986 the *News of the World* published an account of a bizarre encounter between Michael Stacpoole, Archer's "fixer" and Ms Coughlan on Platform 3 of Victoria Station in which Stacpoole offered her an envelope stuffed with £50.00 notes to leave the country. Miss Coughlan was wearing a wire. No allegation of payment for sex was made in the article but its implication caused Archer to resign as Deputy Chairman of the Conservative Party. On November 2nd the *Daily Star* alleged that Archer had paid Coughlan for "perverted sex". On November 5th, Archer issued a writ for libel and won.'

Paul Kelso, the *Guardian*, 20th July 2001

"I did not have sexual relations with that woman"

US President Bill Clinton, under oath, defining his relationship with White House intern Monica Lewinsky in 1999.

President Clinton later apologized to the American people. He had claimed that as full sexual intercourse did not take place, he was not lying when he described his intensely physical relationship with Miss Lewinsky in this manner

'I have never, I repeat never, met Monica Coughlan or had any association of any kind with a prostitute,' He [Jeffrey Archer] insisted...

Daily Mail, 20th July 2001 reporting on the trial of Jeffrey Archer for perjury, recalling Lord Archer's statements in1987 in connection with his suit against the *Daily Star* for libel.

What's the difference?

Jeffrey Archer

A. Alleged philanderer.

B. Told lies, in court, under oath.

C. Involved in a sex scandal with a woman called Monica.

D. Doing time in Her Majesty's Prison.

What's the difference?

Bill Clinton

A. Alleged philanderer.

B. Told lies, in court, under oath.

C. Involved in a sex scandal with a woman called Monica.

D. Doing a world tour, promoting his memoirs.

Inspired by *Private Eye*, 27th July 2001

'I didn't inhale it.'

1992: Governor Bill Clinton, when he was a candidate for the Presidency, attempting to limit the damage to his Presidential chances when he had been forced to acknowledge that he had 'experimented once or twice' with marijuana when he had been at college.

'It isn't pollution that's harming our environment. It's impurities in our air and water that's doing it.'

Former US Vice President Dan Quayle

'[Archer's lies] also secured him a place at Dover College, a small public school in Kent, where he worked before going to Oxford... A CV claim to a BSc still exists in the Dover school archive.'

Andrew Pierce *The Times*,
20th July 2001

'Of all the treasures a State can
possess, the human lives of its
citizens are for us the most precious.'

Joseph Stalin, Soviet dictator.
In the years between 1930 and 1938 it is
estimated that Stalin was responsible for
the deaths of twenty to forty million Soviet
citizens. He called for mass executions and
induced famines to punish uncooperative
regions and opponents of his dictatorship

'At Oxford he flourished at athletics. He [Archer] ran for England, but even that honour had to be embroidered. He subsequently claimed to have represented his country at the Olympic Games – another outrageous and easily checkable fact.'

The Times, 20th July 2001

'The movement is not a Communist movement. We have no intention of expropriating US property, and any property we take we'll pay for.'

Communist revolutionary Fidel Castro, on his intentions after seizing power in Cuba in 1959

Jeffrey Archer's entry in *Who's Who* contained a string of falsehoods. In 2000, he was forced to remove a claim that he was the patron of the Youth Sports Trust, a charity which helps children of all abilities to take part in sport.

He also removed a false entry claiming he was the honorary president of a Glasgow University student debating society.

The *Independent* 2nd August 2001

'The Sudetenland is the last territorial claim I have to make in Europe.'

Adolf Hitler, Chancellor of Germany, outlining the limits to his plans for domination in Europe in 1938. Before a year had passed he invaded Poland, leading directly to the outbreak of the Second World War

Roll of Shame

Jeffrey Archer joins other top politicians on a roll of shame now that he is serving a prison sentence:

Horatio Bottomley: Independent MP for South Hackney, jailed in 1922 for seven years for embezzlement

Jonathan Aitken: Conservative MP for Thanet South and ex Cabinet minister, jailed in 1999 for eighteen months for perjury.

John Stonehouse: Labour MP for Walsall North and ex-Postmaster-General: sentenced to seven years in 1976 for theft and false pretences

Peter Baker: Tory MP for South Norfolk; sentenced to seven years in 1954 for forgery

'They were inventions, nothing was true… There is nothing true about these allegations. They are as untrue as everything else that these people have been telling in the past.'

In 1986 former UN Secretary-General Kurt Waldheim campaigned to be President of Austria. The World Jewish Congress had discovered documents proving that Waldheim had been part of a Nazi unit which had in turn been involved in war atrocities in the years after 1941. Waldheim's official biography claimed that he was wounded in this year and spent the remainder of the war studying law in Vienna

Rearranging the truth:

Anagrams

'Jeffrey Archer, Novelist'

Clever Tory? Ha! Sniff! Jeer!

The *Daily Express*
www.AnagramGenius.com

Pensioners mugged by men in suits

When Robert Maxwell was found to have fiddled the Mirror Group pension fund, he was posthumously branded a robber baron.

'Your pension is safe with me', intoned the voice of Robert Maxwell in a Mirror Group in-house video in 1988. A month after his mysterious death on 5th November 1991, it emerged that £480m had been siphoned out of the pension funds of various companies in the Maxwell empire.'

Andrew Calcutt, *Living Marxism*

A TWIST IN THE TALE

true or false?

Rearranging the truth: Anagrams

'Lord Archer of Weston-super-Mare'

Oh Dear Me! Sorrowful Creep Rants
Robin Hill

Adulterer romps on whores? Farce!
Anon

Oh Wonderful Smartarse or creep?
Donald L. Holmes
www.AnagramGenius.com

What's in a name?

Steveland Morris Hardaway	=	Stevie Wonder
Edna Ruston	=	Audrey Hepburn
Khrishna Bhanji	=	Ben Kingsley
Ehrich Weiss	=	Harry Houdini
William Bailey	=	Axl Rose
Caryn Johnson	=	Whoopi Goldberg
Joyce Frankenberg	=	Jane Seymour

Jeffrey Archer has shown some prescience in the choice of titles during his very successful writing career. Here are a few to conjure with:

Kane and Abel

A Matter of Honour

Not a Penny More, Not a Penny Less

Twelve Red Herrings

A Twist in the Tale

Honour among Thieves

Beyond Reasonable Doubt

Expert Witness

The Accused

Sebastian Melmoth

When he was released from prison in 1897 the celebrated playwright and socialite Oscar Wilde ran away to Paris, where he remained in exile until his death. To avoid further ignominy after his imprisonment for homosexual acts he used his *nom de plume* 'Sebastian Melmoth'. Although every detail was accounted for even down to monogramming his luggage with 'S.M.' he was such a well known and distinctive man, tall, with long flowing hair and an eccentric wardrobe, that the alias was pointless.

Monica Coughlan, the prostitute at the heart of the 1987 trial for libel against the *Daily Star*, claimed that Jeffrey Archer had told her that he was a second-hand car dealer after their ten-minute encounter.

'That is not a lie, it's a terminological inexactitude'

Former US Secretary of State Alexander Haig, defending himself against accusations of lying in 1983

The alleged encounter between Archer and Monica Coughlan 'saw him engineer a complex criminal conspiracy, forge his diaries, procure false alibis and corrupt those around him. He sacrificed the probity and reputation of his wife, his mistress, his personal assistant and several friends to save himself at the high court in 1987.'

Paul Kelso, the *Guardian,* 20th July, 2001

A QUIVER FULL OF ARROWS

fibs and falsehoods

'I didn't solicit anybody.'

Eddie Murphy, assuring the police that there was a mistake, when they caught him with a twenty-year-old transvestite prostitute on Santa Monica Boulevard, L.A. in 1987. Sex was not on his mind. Murphy claimed he had gone out to buy a newspaper and, acting kindly, had simply offered the prostitute a lift. He was not arrested; the prostitute was.

Accused of lying by Archer's counsel during the libel action she [Monica Coughlan] said, "He's the liar… Do you know what I've been through for that liar? Just because he's got power and money."

The *Guardian*, 20th July 2001

A LIAR'S
OF TRUT

MOMENT

'On 19th July 2001, Jeffrey Archer was found guilty at the Old Bailey of two counts of perjury and two of perverting the course of justice and sentenced to four years in prison. 'The judge spoke of the way he had preyed upon the weak and vulnerable to concoct his alibis; the way he hurried along the original libel trial to tell his lies and spin his fabrications.'

Simon Hoggart, the *Guardian*,
20th July 2001

'I have no weakness for shoes. I wear very simple shoes.'

After the fall of the dictatorship of her husband, President Marcos of the Philippines, in 1986, 3,400 pairs of very fancy footwear indeed were discovered in First Lady's Imelda Marcos's wardrobes: at Malacanang Palace.

The prostitute:

'Monica Coughlan, the prostitute at the centre of the libel action in 1987 against the *Daily Star* newspaper, was the greatest victim of Jeffrey Archer's lies.

'According to Mr Justice Caulfield, the trial judge on that occasion, Ms Coughlan provided 'cold, unloving, rubber-insulated sex in a seedy hotel room'.

'Ms Coughlan stood by her story that Archer had paid her for sex, until her death in a car accident, fourteen years later in April 2001.

'Monica answered Archer's counsel when he accused her of lying, with counter-accusations that Archer was lying.

"You might be big with words, OK, and I might be just a prostitute, but I've never harmed anybody, OK? I've just survived all my life? He knows that it's him, he knows it."' Monica was dogged for the rest of her life by being branded a liar when Archer won his libel case against the *Daily Star*.'

The *Guardian*, 20th July 2001

'I haven't committed a crime. What I did was fail to comply with the law.'

David Dinkins, New York City Mayor

The secretary:

'Angela Peppiatt, was a "reluctant assassin." She was Jeffrey Archer's personal assistant during the 1987 libel action . . . she organized payments to Michael Stacpoole, the 'fixer' who contacted Monica Coughlan with inducements to leave the country. She also bought and forged a false diary on Archer's behalf, to confirm in court that he had appointments elsewhere when it was alleged that he had met with the prostitute Monica Coughlan. Ms Peppiatt kept copies of the forged diary, which were used as vital evidence at Archer's trial in 2001 for perjury and perverting the course of justice.'

The *Guardian,* 20th July 2001

Ten lies husbands tell their wives

1   You've no reason to be jealous
2   It'll never happen again
3   It was just that one time
4   I thought you knew
5   I never meant for this to happen
6   She seduced me
7   I was drunk
8   I don't even remember her name
9   It meant nothing to me
10   You know that it is you I love

The mistress:

'Andrina Colquhoun was Archer's mistress. She was proof of Archer's infidelity. Ted Francis' false alibi on Archer's behalf in 1987 was, he believed, designed to protect Archer's marriage, as Archer claimed he had been dining with Andrina on the night he was alleged to have paid Monica Coughlan for sex. Ted Francis and Andrina Colquhoun were deceived by Archer's mendacity, but Francis blew the whistle on Archer when the latter announced his candidacy as Mayor of London. Francis felt that Lord Archer was unsuitable to stand for high office and revealed his part in Lord Archer's fabrications in 1987. This led directly to Archer's trial for perjury in July 2001.'

The *Guardian,* 20th July 2001

Ten lies married men tell their mistresses

1   I thought you knew
2   She doesn't understand me
3   We have an understanding
4   It hasn't been good for a long time
5   It's not the way it is with you
6   I can't leave while the children are young /
    doing their exams / getting married
7   We've simply grown apart
8   She depends on me, I can't hurt her
9   I'll tell her I'm leaving
10 I can't see you tonight, she's getting suspicious

'Jeffrey Archer had a passion for blondes and cheated on wife Mary for more than twenty years with three fair-haired mistresses.'
Sally Farmiloe, Nikki Kingdon and Andrina Colquhoun

'We are not retreating – we are advancing in another direction.'

US General Douglas Macarthur

'I wasn't lying, Senator. I was presenting a different version from the facts.'

Colonel Oliver North, at the Iran-Contra hearings in 1987

TWELVE
RED
HERRINGS

diversions and digressions

One fishy story

about Lord Archer's father...

Jeffrey Archer has 'claimed many things about his father including that he was British consul in Singapore.' Actually he was a convicted fraudster and bigamist who travelled to the USA on his dead employer's passport. He lived out the war years duping, in the words of a 1919 newspaper article "many well-known New York People." '

Evening Standard, 27th July 2001

Appearances can be deceptive

In 1990, a Colorado Springs High School welcomed a new student to its campus. A bright and popular young lady, Cheyen Weatherley made the all-girl cheerleading squad. Unfortunately, Cheyen was actually a twenty-six–year-old man named Charles Dougherty. It was some time before 'her' records were discovered to be a total fiction. Charles was arrested and charged with criminal impersonation. He served two years' probation, and was required to undergo psychiatric counselling.

Two fishy stories

about school...

Archer attended Wellington School in Somerset. Private, but not, as some may have mistakenly believed, the exclusive public school Wellington College in Berkshire.

'School? Well, I – uh. I was going to
school till I met somebody.

'Yeah! Uh – two big monsters.
And – and they tied me in a big sack!'

Pinocchio – his first lie to his 'father' after
skipping school and the start of his nasal
growth spurt

Three fishy stories

about university...

Archer claims to have been a student at Oxford
University, but according to Michael Crick in his
unauthorized biography, *Stranger Than Fiction,*
he was actually at the less exclusive Oxford
Department of Education, which is affiliated to
the University.

True lies

schooldays

Please excuse R from P.E. for a few days. Yesterday he fell out of a tree and misplaced his hip.

My daughter was absent from school yesterday because she spent the weekend with the marines and was exhausted.

Please excuse E. from school today. She was sick and I had her shot.

Four fishy stories

more about university...

Lord Archer's entry in *Who's Who* still lists
Brasenose College as his alma mater. Although
the Oxford Department of Education is affiliated
to the University, it is alleged that he gave false
academic qualifications to get on the course,
including three non-existent A levels.

True lies

Excuses excuses

Please excuse R from school. He has very loose vowels.

Please excuse A for missing school today. We forgot to get the Sunday paper off the mat, and when we found it on Monday, we thought it was Sunday.

Please excuse F for being absent yesterday. He had diarrhoea and his boots leak.

Five fishy stories

Archer claimed that he had become a fellow of
the International Federation of Physical Culture
following his two-year course at the University of
California. The Federation was a London-based
correspondence course in body-building.

Ten lies children tell about school

1 A bigger boy did it
2 I haven't got any homework
3 The dog ate my homework
4 We are going to study the whole time
5 It's a study day
6 I left it at school
7 There was no letter
8 The teacher said the test was cancelled
9 The teacher was really pleased with me
10 Big boys took my homework and threw it in the dustbin

Six fishy stories

Occupation?

In 1966, Jeffrey Archer married Mary Weedon, who accurately described herself on her marriage certificate as a 'research graduate', as did her husband, though he was not.

Names, names, names

Rodent operative   rat catcher

Cleanliness executive   cleaner

Domestic goddess/god   housewife/husband

Strategic vehicle
positioning officer   parking attendant

External/internal viewing
medium cleanliness executive   window cleaner

Waste disposal operative   dustbin man/woman

Seven fishy stories

Nothing to Hide?

On 6th October 1999. Archer defeated Steven Norris by 15,716 votes to 6,350 to win the Tory candidacy for London mayor, but was forced to resign in November 1999 when the *News of the World* reported that he persuaded a former friend, Ted Francis, to lie in court in the 1987 libel trial.

Only months earlier, Archer had assured the Tory Party chairman, Michael Ancram, that there were no more damaging allegations about him which could resurface.

Ten occupational lies

1 I'm sure we agreed that you would do it
2 I wasn't at that meeting
3 Who's been moving things on my desk?
4 He's in a meeting
5 She's on the other line
6 It's under control
7 Our profits aren't as high as we expected
8 Industry does not exist solely to make a profit
9 My door is always open
10 What's good for the business is good for you

Eight fishy stories

'Parliament? he should be in a remand home!'

Humphry Berkeley, MP on whether Jeffrey Archer was a
suitable parliamentary candidate, 1969

Ten social lies

1   You know I would if I could
2   I know exactly what you mean
3   Well they didn't find out from me
4   I'd forgotten all about it
5   It's no trouble at all
6   No I don't think you over reacted
7   In your position, I'd do exactly the
    same thing
8   Of course you may say you were with me
9   I would love it, but I have a previous
    engagement
10 It doesn't matter, it wasn't valuable

'We do not have censorship. What we have is a limitation of what newspapers can report.'

The South African Deputy Minister for Information, 1987

News of the World
29th July 2001

Nine fishy stories

Four guilty verdicts

Number ONE
PERVERTING THE COURSE OF JUSTICE

'Procuring Ted Francis to provide an alibi, which he knew to be false and which was intended to disprove the allegation in the 1987 libel action'.
VERDICT July 2001 GUILTY

Ten fishy stories

Four guilty verdicts

Number TWO
PERVERTING THE COURSE OF JUSTICE

'Failing to disclose the existence of his main office diary for 1986: providing Angela Peppiatt, his personal assistant with a blank 1986 diary and instructing her to write entries in it; and causing the diary to be handed to his solicitors for use in the court case as his main office diary.'
VERDICT July 2001 GUILTY

In 1906, referring to the government's denials of the exploitation of Chinese coolies in South Africa, he said, 'Perhaps we have been guilty of some terminological inexactitudes.'

Winston Churchill

Eleven fishy stories

Four guilty verdicts

Number THREE
PERJURY

'Making a statement under oath for use in judicial proceedings that the *Economist Diary* 1986, the appointments diary for 1986 and a list of appointments for 1986 were the only documents of that type which had been in his possession.'
VERDICT July 2001 GUILTY

Winston Churchill said of Stanley Baldwin: 'He occasionally stumbled over the truth, but hastily picked himself up and hurried on as if nothing had happened.' Interestingly, Baldwin said that Churchill 'cannot really tell lies. That is what makes him so bad a conspirator.'

Twelve fishy stories

Four guilty verdicts

Number FOUR
PERJURY

'Knowingly making a false statement as a sworn witness in the High Court, that the diary known as the main diary or Mrs Peppiatt's diary produced in proceedings was in existence and contained the entries relating to September 8th and 9th 1986, before October 26th 1986.
VERDICT July 2001 GUILTY

BEYOND REASONABLE DOUBT

on lies, liars and lying

'There are a terrible lot of lies going around the world, and the worst of it is half of them are true.'

Winston Churchill

Hello, hello, hello... What's going on here then?

Curiously, Jeffrey Archer does not acknowledge that he spent some time in the Metropolitan Police force, although a photograph of him exists in uniform, attesting to his service to the community.

'Sometimes truth is so precious, it must be attended by a bodyguard of lies.'

Winston Churchill, speaking at the Tehran Conference in 1943, was referring specifically to Allied plans for the invasion of Europe. (In the event Operation Overlord, the codename for the brilliantly successful Normandy landings in June 1944, was attended, and in many respects made possible, by a series of imaginative and astonishingly effective deception operations – or 'lies'.)

A charming fraud, without the charm

'It was in the late 1960's that Humphry Berkeley asked me whether I had ever heard of Jeffrey Archer…

…'I said I had indeed heard of him…

…'But, I said to Berkeley, I had never had the pleasure of meeting him. That was odd, Berkeley replied. In his expenses form Archer claimed to have bought me lunch only a few weeks before. I was puzzled and slightly perturbed, for it is not pleasant to figure in the expenses claim of someone you have never set eyes on in your life.

'A few weeks later Berkeley produced for my inspection an incriminating dossier of Archer's delinquencies. The curious thing was the smallness of the sums involved, hardly worth a false claim... Still, Berkeley decided he was unfit to become a Tory MP, the career Archer was then pursuing. Berkeley was a determined and could be a vindictive enemy... He certainly wrote to Anthony Barber, the party chairman. It was to no avail. In 1969, following a by-election, Archer entered the House as Member for Louth.'

Alan Watkins, The *Independent*, 24th July 2001

'...Lord McAlpine put it perfectly when explaining why it was that so many of the alleged great and putatively good were taken in by Archer: "Politicians are the easiest people to con because they want to believe in appearances."

'It is ordinary people who are in a position to reveal the truth about the Archers of this world, because they are not offered the appearances. They get the reality.'

...In the early 1990s I was on a literary tour in the US. In Portland, Oregon, my escort (the person responsible for driving the writer from interview to book-signing to interview) told me that when she had finished escorting Archer, she felt so emotionally destroyed and personally demeaned that she had got in touch with all the escorts she knew of who had been dealing with him in other cities. Together, they had then instituted the "I Survived Jeffrey Archer Club", which issued its own memorabilia, T-shirts and fountain pens bearing the above slogan.'

Will Self, *The Sociopath*, The *Independent,* 20th July 2001

'A little sincerity is a dangerous thing, and a great deal of it is absolutely fatal.'

Oscar Wilde,
Intentions: The Critic as Artist

'I hope you have not been leading a double life, pretending to be wicked and really being good all the time. That would be hypocrisy'.

Oscar Wilde, *The Importance of Being Earnest*

'In its way this is typical of the Archer approach to life. He tells lies not only to avoid uncomfortable truths but apparently for the hell of it. As a first, rather than a last, resort. Then, having convinced himself of the truth of his inventions, he seems genuinely upset to be challenged.'

Clive Anderson, the *Guardian*, 22nd July 2001, on a television interview he conducted with Jeffrey Archer in 1991

'He will lie even when it is inconvenient: the sign of a true artist.'

Attributed to Gore Vidal, American novelist and critic

' Jeffrey Archer's career has consisted largely of getting into "scrapes", as Margaret Thatcher indulgently called them, and getting out of them again; but he is surely too discredited, and too old, ever to get fully clear of this one. Perhaps he will write a book, a play, a film based loosely, in order to avoid the seizure of profits from his crime – on his experience of prison.
But it is to be hoped that he will go to his dotage a discredited man...'

The *Independent*, 24th July 2001

'he is asked to stand, he wants to sit, he is expected to lie.'

Winston Churchill

'The flamboyant Tory peer and millionaire novelist's luck finally ran out when TV producer Ted Francis decided to kiss-and-sell for just enough money to replace his clapped-out D-reg Audi with a new set of wheels (£14,000). The best-selling author's downfall was triggered when Mr Francis decided to tell the bizarre 1987 tale of the alibi that never was to the *News of the World.*'

Mr Francis has said that he had to make his statement when Archer decided to stand for Mayor of London

'He disclosed that Archer persuaded him in January 1987 to write a letter to Archer's lawyers falsely stating they had dinner together on September 9 the previous year, and the Tory even changed his diary to show a meeting.
The *Daily Star* had claimed Archer slept with Coughlan in a cheap London hotel that night, and the author maintained he wanted to protect the identity of a "close personal friend" - former assistant Andrina Colquhoun, with whom he dined. Mr Francis agreed to cover over a meal in Sambuca, a small Italian bistro off Sloane Square.

"I'm not proud of it, "he said, "but that's the bald truth. I lied for a good friend because he asked me."

The *Guardian*

'One of the striking differences between a cat and a lie is that the cat has only nine lives.'

Mark Twain

'Jeffrey Archer is a candidate of probity and integrity.'

As said by William Hague on *Channel 4 News*, 1999, with reference to Jeffrey Archer's bid to become Mayor of London

'There's a real love of a lie, Liars find ready-made for lies they make As hand for glove, or tongue for sugarplum.'

Robert Browning, 1864

Lies Jeffrey told me

'Then came the first lie. By this time I was working as a foreign correspondent in New York and I was asked to follow up a tip-off that Archer, now an MP, was in Las Vegas negotiating to bring Elvis Presley to perform in Britain. I rang the Desert Sands Hotel and asked for him. He answered the phone, confirmed it was him and I stated my business. There was a pause. "Gee," he said. "You gat the wrong man. I'm Jeffrey Archer from Cali-fornia." It was a dreadful accent, but he wouldn't budge. I rang the hotel again, asked for Reservations and politely asked them to confirm that it was a Mr Jeffrey with a 'J' Archer who was a guest in the hotel. It was. From London? That's right. I wrote a story saying that Archer was pretending not to be in Las Vegas and my newspaper put it on the front page.'

Julia Langdon, the *Guardian,* 9th December, 1999

'The most common lie is that which one lies to himself; lying to others is relatively an exception.'

Friedrich Nietzsche

"I will at all times try to live up to the reputation of your lordships' House as expressed so eloquently by the Scottish bard:

"Princes and Lords are but the breath of Kings. An honest man is the noblest work of God.'"

Jeffrey Archer: his maiden speech to the House of Lords in 1992, quoting Robert Burns

'The liar at any rate recognizes that recreation, not instruction, is the aim of conversation, and is a far more civilized being than the blockhead who loudly expresses his disbelief in a story which is told simply for the amusement of the company.'

Oscar Wilde

'To his friends and acquaintances,
spinning tales
was just part of Lord Archer's
unusual charm –
until it all got rather out of hand...'

Julia Langdon, the *Guardian*,
9th December 1999

'With lies you may go ahead in the world, but you can never go back.'

Russian proverb

'No lying knight or lying priest ever prospered in any age, but especially not in the dark ones. Men prospered then only in following an openly declared purpose, and preaching candidly beloved and trusted creeds.'

John Ruskin

'ARCHER IS A TEA BOY IN PRISON'

'Jailed Lord Archer has landed work as a TEA BAG monitor in tough Belmarsh jail. The millionaire peer, 61, goes from cell to cell on his third-floor wing handing out each inmate's daily ration of one bag – and has been warned he must stop tea leafs swiping extra supplies…

… '"All his money and influence count for nothing here. And woe betide him if a lag blags an extra bag" (A Belmarsh source)'

Nick Parker, the *Sun*, 31st July 2001

'Whoever is detected in a shameful fraud is ever after not believed even if they speak the truth.'

Phaedrus

'ARCH MOANER'

'Jailed Jeffrey has been locked up between two killers after moaning about the size of his cell…
A prison source said: "Archer was furious.
He kept walking up and down saying, "I'm 61 years old, and I'm made to share a cell two paces wide by four paces long. It really is taking a liberty".
One of the guys told him, "No, this is a loss of liberty" – that shut him up for a while."'

The *Mirror*, 1st August, 2001

'Every violation of truth is not only a sort of suicide in the liar, but is a stab at the health of human society.'

Ralph Waldo Emerson

'Archer cannot be trusted in an open prison'

'Lord Archer of Weston-super-Mare was yesterday reclassified as a prisoner who cannot be trusted to be sent to an open jail. [Lord Archer]… was informed of the decision at Belmarsh, the top security prison near Woolwich in southeast London, where he has been held since being convicted [of perjury and conspiracy to pervert the course of justice.]'

'Hazel Banks, the Governor of the jail, took the decision to place Archer, 61, in a higher risk category after it was disclosed that police are looking at a complaint relating to the whereabouts of £57 million that the author claimed was collected by the Simple Truth fundraising campaign to help the Iraqi Kurds in 1991.'

Richard Ford, *The Times*, 1st August 2001

'The liar's punishment is, not in the least that he cannot be believed, but that he cannot believe anyone else.'

George Bernard Shaw